Little Pebble™

Farm Facts

T0025414

Animals
on the Farm

by Lisa J. Amstutz

PEBBLE
a capstone imprint

Pebble Books are published by Pebble
1710 Roe Crest Drive
North Mankato, Minnesota 56003
www.mycapstone.com

Library of Congress Cataloging-in-Publication Data
is available on the Library of Congress website.
ISBN 978-1-9771-0256-0 (library binding)
ISBN 978-1-9771-0536-3 (paperback)
ISBN 978-1-9771-0261-4 (eBook PDF)
Summary: Introduces beginning readers to seven
of the most common animals on a farm. Up-close
photos and leveled text pair up for a fun meet-
and-greet filled with facts, feathers, and fur.

Editorial Credits
Jill Kalz, editor; Ashlee Suker, designer;
Kelly Garvin, media researcher;
Katy LaVigne, production specialist

Photo Credits
iStockphoto/pixdeluxe, 5; Shutterstock: Anastasija
Popova, 13, bagicat, 1 (right), Baronb, cover,
BIGANDT.COM, 19, jadimages, 1 (left), Julia
Lototskaya, 10, kevin leah, 15, Leo D, 8,
monticello, 14, photoshooter2015, 21, r.classen,
backcover, 6, sixpixx, 16, smereka, 7, 9, talseN,
11, William John Hunter, 17, yevgeniy11, 20

Design Element
Shutterstock: Dudarev Mikhail, J.Schelkle,
K.Narloch-Liberra, laura.h, Sichon

Table of Contents

Living Together

Farmers and their families live on farms. Who else lives there? Animals! Let's meet them.

Making Milk

Hello, cows!

Cows make milk.

They eat grain, hay,
and grass.

Hello, goats!

Goats make milk too.

They have horns and

long ears.

Sharing the Farm

Hello, pigs! Pigs have snouts and curly tails. They roll in mud to keep cool.

Hello, horses!
Horses have long,
strong legs. They can
run fast.

Hello, chickens!

Chickens lay eggs.

Maybe a chick
will hatch!

Hello, sheep!

Sheep grow wool.

It is warm and soft.

Hello, dogs!

Some dogs herd sheep.

They keep them safe.

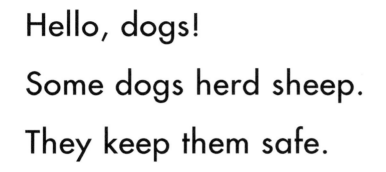

Goodbye, farm animals!

Moo! Maa! Oink! Neigh!

Cluck! Baa! Woof!

Glossary

grain—the seed of a grassy plant such as wheat, rice, corn, rye, or barley

hatch—to break out of an egg

hay—dried field grasses

herd—to gather animals into a group

neigh—the sound a horse makes

snout—the long, front part of an animal's head, including the nose, mouth, and jaws

wool—the soft, thick, curly hair of sheep or goats; wool is used to make yarn

Read More

Hall, Margaret. *Cows and Their Calves: A 4D Book.* Animal Offspring. North Mankato, Minn.: Capstone Press, a Capstone imprint, 2018.

Lynch, Annabelle. *Farm Animals.* Nature Explorers. New York: Windmill Books, 2016.

Mattern, Joanne. *Farm Animals.* National Geographic Kids Readers. Washington, D.C.: National Geographic, 2017.

Internet Sites

Use FactHound to find Internet sites related to this book.

Visit *www.facthound.com*

Just type in 9781977102560 and go.

Super-cool stuff! Check out projects, games and lots more at **www.capstonekids.com**

Critical Thinking Questions

1. What are two farm animals in this book that make milk?

2. Why do pigs roll in mud?

3. How do some dogs help farmers?

Index